E

ER

Collected by Barrie Wade
Illustrated by Steve Smallman

Collins Educational
An Imprint of HarperCollins*Publishers*

Why was the teacher cross-eyed?

She couldn’t control her pupils.

What do you call a
gorilla with an axe?

Sir.

What did the sea say to the sand?

Nothing. It just waves.

Why did the burglar
stop to have a bath?

So he could make a clean getaway.

What do frogs like to drink?

Croaker-Cola.

What is the best musical instrument?

A drum takes a lot of beating.

What do you get if you cross a hen with a cement mixer?

A brick layer.